Malaika Kegode

Outlier

T0272732

Salamander Street

PLAYS

First published in 2021 by Salamander Street Ltd.

(info@salamanderstreet.com)

Outlier © Malaika Kegode, 2021

ISBN: 9781914228339

10 9 8 7 6 5 4 3 2 1

INTRODUCTION BY BEN ATTERBURY

My journey with *Outlier* begins sometime in 2019, sitting in the Tobacco Factory Theatre in Bristol attending one of Malaika's Milk poetry nights - because not only is Malaika an extraordinary writer and performer, she's also an incredible cultural organiser, providing a platform for so many other poets in Bristol & the rest of the UK.

I've been invited to come and watch Malaika and Jakabol play together. They've been working together for a while now, fusing Malaika's rich and emotive poetry with Jakabol's melodic intensity. I've been invited because they are thinking about making a theatre show, even though they've never made one before & they aren't sure how they'll do it; I'm excited about that. I'm more excited by the time they finish playing because it's obvious to absolutely everyone in the room that there is something very, very special about this collaboration. As it would happen, I'm sitting near Jenny Davies, who has also been invited to watch the show and talk to the team about directing it. Jenny and I have already been working together for some time, and watching Malaika and Jakabol I know her brilliant talents and fantastic instincts are exactly what this collaboration needs and it's more exciting all over again. I leave, knowing I'm going to help them make this show in whatever way I can.

One of the great joys of working in this field is watching artists unlock their potential and walk through a door that's just opened. We've had that many times with *Outlier*; the project develops and unlocks a little more, we head through a door together and on the other side the team of people cheering this project on is bigger and louder than before.

This project is a celebration of friendship – onstage and off – showing how it is possible to face our biggest and darkest challenges, as long as we have their support & their love. It's been a great privilege to help discover the ways that Malaika can share her tender words with us. Her story within these pages is a gift; read it and imagine it performed with love, heart and loud, loud music on stage by five brilliant and talented friends & their many incredibly talented collaborators and friends who helped them make it.

Outlier was first performed at Bristol Old Vic on 12 June 2021.

Written and performed by **Malaika Kegode**

With original music written and performed by **Jakabol**

Director **Jenny Davies**

Producer **Liz Counsell**

Designer **Rebecca Wood**

Animation and Projection Design **Christopher Harrisson**

Lighting Design **Joe Price**

Associate Designer **Alana Ashley**

Assistant Producer **Sophie Power**

Dramaturgy Support **Marietta Kirkbride**

Artist Wellbeing **Lou Platt**

Stage Management **Cassie Harrison**

Marketing Outreach Associate **Sarah Papworth**

Projection Consultant **Tom Newell**

Vocal Coach **Dom Coyote**

Photography **Paul Blakemore**

Bristol Old Vic Ferment Producer **Ben Atterbury**

Bristol Old Vic Production Manager **Jemma Edwards**

CAST

Malaika Kegode – MAL

Malaika is a writer, performer and producer based in Bristol. She has performed around the UK at a number of celebrated venues, festivals and literary events including The 100 Club, WOMAD and Edinburgh Book Festival. Her writing has been published in multiple anthologies, and her two poetry collections *Requite* (2017) and *Thalassic* (2020) are published by Burning Eye Books. In addition to her own writing, Malaika is a poetry mentor and workshop leader, she is passionate about helping people build their confidence and tell their own stories.

Outside of poetry, Malaika has had essays published around themes of culture, film and race, and has also worked as a programme selector for Encounters Film Festival and Tallinn Black Nights.

Marietta Kirkbride – HOLLY

Marietta is a writer, theatre-maker and violinist based in Bristol. She has fifteen years of experience performing and composing for electric violin with bands, ranging from post-metal to folk, and has played in pubs and bars in Bristol, Birmingham and Worcestershire. As a theatre-maker, she has performed violin at venues and festivals including Arcola Theatre, Bristol Old Vic, Latitude Festival, Wilderness Festival and Lyric Hammersmith Theatre in the Square.

As a writer, Marietta's work has been produced by Radio 4, Watermill Theatre, Theatre West and in association with Bucket Club.

Joe Williams – OSKAR, PARTY GOERS

Joe is a multi-instrumentalist based in Bristol. He is co-founder of Jakabol and bassist for Neo-soul group Pahla. With influences spanning from John McLaughlin to MF DOOM, Joe is passionate about fusing and exploring musical landscapes to stretch the limits of genre. His eclectic style has seen him perform around the country, and collaborate with artists across disciplines. In addition to his live performance, Joe is a drama graduate who has been scoring theatre and film since 2011. He is always searching for new ways of telling stories through sound.

On the rare occasion he is not making music, Joe can be found brewing for Bristol's Left Handed Giant brewery.

Emmy Broughton – AMA

Emmy feels passionate about making music for stories that initiate social change. Combining music with mental health awareness feels essential to her artistic journey, and she is hopeful that *Outlier* will lead to change happening in the lives of people who see the show.

Since leaving school Emmy has explored various creative roles in community groups and performance projects. Her time in Bristol started twelve years ago, running an allotment project to support asylum seekers and refugees in connecting to nature and producing local food. She has also participated in the Workshare program for Sims Hill Shared Harvest since the CSA formed in 2011. Emmy went from allotments to forest school and led groups of children exploring the woods in South East Bristol.

All these elements combine to motivate Emmy in making music to support land rights, people's well-being, and their connection to nature.

Owen Gatley – LEWIS, AMA'S DAD

Owen is a musician and illustrator hailing from Worcestershire, now living in Bristol. As a musician, he has over fifteen years of experience writing and performing guitar and drums in various projects and genres, including experimental progressive metal, indie, post-hardcore, and with his current band, Jakabol, folk prog-rock.

He works as an illustrator with editorial and commercial clients including *The Guardian*, BBC, Adidas and Waitrose.

Jakabol

Fusing world folk influences with progressive textures and explosive riffs, Jakabol are an experimental music collective based in Bristol. Inspired by the cinematic energy of bands like Mahavishnu Orchestra and King Gizzard and The Lizard Wizard, they find chaotic beauty in the dichotomy of their eclectic lineup. Jakabol's full lineup is Joe Williams (guitar), Emmy Broughton (harp), Owen Gatley (drums), Luke Saxton (keys) and Marietta Kirkbride (violin).

CREATIVES

Jenny Davies

Jenny Davies is a Bristol-based director and theatre-maker. In 2019 she was awarded a prestigious Leverhulme Arts Scholarship through Bristol Old Vic. She was resident Assistant Director at Tobacco Factory Theatres 2018/19, assisting Nik Partridge on *The Borrowers*, adapted by Bea Roberts, and then assisting Mike Tweddle on *A Midsummer Night's Dream* and co-directing *The Things We Carry*. In 2019 Jenny directed Papatango prize-winning writer Samuel Bailey's play *The Waiting Room*, and *Basset* by James Graham at The Egg, Theatre Royal Bath. She is co-founder of Propolis Theatre, a company formed out of the Bristol Old Vic Made in Bristol programme and a member of Interval artists collective.

Liz Counsell

Liz is an experienced Creative Producer and Arts Consultant with over ten years of experience working across multiple art forms. She has worked in both strategic and delivery roles with Trinity Bristol, MAYK, Tongue Fu, Roundhouse, BBC Arts and Radio 1Xtra and is the Co-Director of Disability Arts Festival I'm Here, Where Are You?

Liz's work centres around artist development, community engagement, social prescribing and creating accessible experiences that share lived experiences with a wide range of audiences.

Rebecca Wood

Rebecca is a designer for performance-based in Bristol. She was the recipient of the Leverhulme Scholarship at Bristol Old Vic 2019/20 and a Linbury Finalist in 2015. Founder of the Bristol Design Assembly and a founding member of theatre company Bucket Club. She has been working with Alana Ashley on this project while she has been on maternity leave.

Credits include *Pinocchio* (Gloucester Guildhall), *Paradise Planet* (English Touring Opera), *Ask Me Anything* (Newcastle Live) *Out of Sorts* (Theatre503), *Fel Anifail* (Sherman Theatre); *The Flop* (Hijinx & Spymonkey – UK Tour); *Goldfish Bowl* (Paper Birds feat. Caleb Femi at Battersea Arts Centre); *Fossils* (UK Tour, 59E59 New York); *Lorraine & Alan* (Bucket Club for UK Tour).

Joe Price

Joe trained at the Royal Welsh College of Music and Drama and is now based in Bristol. He received the 2015 Francis Reid Award for Lighting Design.

Credits include: *My Name Is Rachel Corrie* (Young Vic), *The World's Wife* (Welsh National Opera), *Redefining Juliet* (Barbican), *Rapunzel* (The Egg, TRB), *Heads Will Roll* (Told by an Idiot), *Heather* (Bush Theatre), *Quality Street* (Northern Broadsides), *Ask Me Anything* (Paper Birds), *What Songs May Do* (Dance City), *Kite* (The Wrong Crowd), *Conditionally* (Soho Theatre), *Mrs Dalloway* (Arcola Theatre), *Father Figurine* (Wardrobe Theatre), *Box Clever* and *Killymuck* (Bunker Theatre), *Fossils* (Brits off Broadway NYC), *Peter Pan* (Barn Theatre), *Frankie Vah* (Luke Wright), *This Must Be the Place* (VAULT Festival), *Let the Right One In* (Arts Ed), *Magnificence* (Finborough Theatre), *Some Girl(s)* (Park Theatre), *Around The World in 80 Days* (Theatre Royal Winchester), *Alternative Routes* (National Dance Company Wales), *Animal/Endless Ocean* (Gate Theatre) and *Y Twr* (Invertigo).

Christopher Harrisson

Christopher Harrisson is an illustrator/animator, writer and theatre-maker, based in Bristol. After training at Ecole Jacques Lecoq he co-founded the award-winning theatre company Rhum and Clay, which he ran from 2011–2016.

Christopher has created illustrations and animations across multiple platforms, with commissions from organisations such as Sony and Selfridges. Animation for theatre includes his solo show *The North! The North!* and the Viking adventure *Vinland* by Jack Dean. Recent animation projects include the computer games *Great North Road* (Jack Dean & Company) and *Truth Sleuth: Thrills, Chills and Chemical Spills* (Modest Genius Theatre Company).

BRISTOL OLD VIC

Bristol Old Vic Ferment is our artist collaboration programme. Every year we work with artists and companies in a variety of ways to support and develop their work and practice. Ferment has been running for over ten years. In that time we've developed a number of artists to make work here in the South West that has then toured nationally and internationally.

We focus our work in two areas:

The Forum, a free and simple to join artist network for any artist in the South West that offers a range of development opportunities and benefits to engage with Bristol Old Vic and other artists in the Forum.

Supported Artists & Companies, individual artists or groups that Ferment invests in to develop work with us, or to develop their practice across scales.

For more details, head to our website.

bristololdvic.org.uk

NOTES ON THE ORIGINAL PRODUCTION

Jenny Davies – Director

Breathe in, breathe out.

When I was growing up, the live performance I would see would be gigs – my mates were in screamo bands that we'd follow each week to Newport or local village halls. We'd spend £2 on the door and cling together in smoky rooms with sticky floors and feel totally alive. When I first read this story, Mal's story, I found myself back there, with my friends, holding on tightly, being thrashed about on the edge of the pit, dodging limbs and sweaty torsos.

The performers in our production have lived this story. You may have lived one like it too. *Outlier* isn't a 'play' sort of a play. We found in rehearsals that, for us, it relies on the honesty of what is happening in the here and now, with whatever audience is present. There is no 'fourth wall', the performers aren't on stage because they were cast after relentless auditions, or because they went to drama school. They are here to help Malaika tell this story, as her friends, who happen to be a band. In our production, the band lent their voices to some of the people in the story, they did this as themselves, speaking lines whilst strapped to a guitar or holding drumsticks.

You may notice throughout reading this text that there are moments of pause (we called these 'Gig Space' moments); they represent a break in the music and the story – Mal and the band would check in with the audience and with each other to see if anyone needs anything, be it water, to tune or perhaps just to take a breath before we continue. I extend this invitation to you; you may be moved or affected by what you find here, if so – go gently and be kind to yourself. In the process of helping Mal tell her story we have all been on a journey together, one of recovery and connection. Mal's story has helped us make sense of our own stories, where we've come from, how we've survived and how we ended up here, right now. I hope it does that for you too.

We wanted our production of *Outlier* to take inspiration from those crowded sweaty gigs and parties, from crashing on landings and falling asleep in bathtubs, from cigarette burns in carpets and wine-stained walls, the morning after de-briefs over cups of tea, jumping ticket barriers at train stations. We wanted it to feel anarchic and loud. But really, *Outlier* is whatever it brings up for you; the moments from your past that this text brings back alive and kicking. We found that this story worked best when you opened up and let it into your bones. Take a deep breath, and follow us in.

Jakabol – Music

We first met Malaika at one of the earlier gigs we played as a full band. She asked if we'd be interested in collaborating, and so we began a process of reworking some of our songs to include her words and wrote new material responding to poems she'd written. Our process ever since has been organic and truly collaborative. Our approach has been to lean into our most raucous riffs while crafting space and emphasis for Malaika's tender and fiercely emotional poetry. For *Outlier*, with Jenny's help, we've continued in this way, challenging the expectations of what a collaboration between a spoken word poet and a band looks like. This is more than a vocalist with a backing band. It's a creative journey between friends and an experiment into what progressive rock can do for storytelling.

Chris Harrisson – Animation and Projection Design

In 2019, Jakabol asked me if I was interested in creating some animations for a short gig they had with Mal. I hadn't done any projection design for music, so was keen to use this as an opportunity to try out some new ideas and techniques. When I was approached about working on *Outlier*, I knew that I could expand on what I'd done and explore some more ambitious territory.

The inspiration for the animation's aesthetic came from various places – teenage doodles, scrapbooks, gig posters – and from Mal, thanks to a treasure trove of photos she generously shared with the creative team. In particular, Ama's bedroom wall, with its scrawl of sharpie scribbles, came to be a central reference point. It felt apt to bring these to life visually, as the show was doing the same for Mal's story.

I was interested in exploring the interplay between abstract with illustrated elements, and how they might sit on the fantastic surfaces and textures provided by Rebecca's design. I have used a variety of digital and analogue techniques to do this, from hand-painted textures to digital drawing, to motion graphics software. It is important to me that the projection supports Mal's story, so I have tried to think of it as another performer in the space, reacting to the music and narrative, playing minor or taking the focus when required.

Rebecca Wood – Designer

Growing up in a Cornish town that isn't too dissimilar to Malaika's Devon home, I found the story in *Outlier* really emotional. It was a story I hadn't seen told on stage before and the combination of Mal's words and Jakabol's music bring real depth and weight to an audience.

I was honoured to be asked to work on this very exciting project and the design came to me relatively instinctively. The world of *Outlier* is both domestic and transcendently epic. I chose a palette of materials that would be familiar to the house and found a way to present them in a way reminiscent of gigs whilst having textured surfaces for Chris' illustrations to project onto.

Joe Price – Lighting Designer

One of the benefits of the current global situation has been an opportunity to reflect and allow for more time to carefully consider decisions in both our work and wider lives. This has certainly been the case for my involvement with *Outlier*. Having not been part of the original R&D, it was a pleasure to be able to offer a fresh perspective on the piece as we held numerous discussions and strived to ensure we were raring to go when lockdown lifted.

I have been fortunate to collaborate with members of the team before, in particular Rebecca. We were keen to present an abstract but recognisable house party setting that was interwoven with a live gig atmosphere, whilst also welcoming the audience into a shared space. We used a wide range of lighting elements, including digital festoon, pendants, table lamps, fairy lights and theatrical lanterns help to include the audience in the world of the play as well as providing a proper gig theatre experience!

Malaika Kegode – Writer

In the process of creating *Outlier*, a routine was formed to support the well-being of the cast. Before each rehearsal, Jenny would lead us in a guided meditation and then give us the space for a check-in. In this time, we could share anything – from our deepest anxieties to what we fancied having for lunch that day. Every morning we laughed, cried, yawned, and formed the foundation for how we would work and hold each other for the rest of the day. The entirety of *Outlier* has felt thoroughly nourishing thanks to a focus on well being – from Jenny's conscious and holistic directing, to an on-call well-being practitioner in the form of Lou Platt who offered one-to-one and group sessions throughout the process. It's quite amazing really, how much making this show has helped me process and re-evaluate just how much of an outlier I have felt throughout my life.

I'm writing this just moments after reading a tribute on Facebook to a girl from my hometown who sadly passed away recently. I've read too many eulogies and tributes like this over the years. As I get older and further away from the experiences I detail in this play, the more I realise how young we were during those difficult times. We are losing young people to isolation and addiction right at the beginning of their stories, and their losses are too often swallowed by their surroundings and circumstances. Young people growing up in rural spaces have such limited resources, their lives are trivialised and parodied or simply ignored.

I wrote *Outlier* to give a legacy to the people I grew up with. I wrote this for the outsiders who grew up in the quiet expanse of the countryside – those who know its darker edges. The working-class kids, the queer kids, the Black kids, the Asian kids, the weird kids, the bad kids, the kids who never made it home.

I wrote this for you. If you need it.

Breathe in, breathe out.

ACKNOWLEDGEMENTS

Luke Saxton, Helen Edwards, Stef O'Driscoll, Emma Williams, Chris Hicks, Joe Spurgeon, Tom Morris, Stewart Pringle, Chelsey Cliff, Matt Graham, Jack Drewry, Amy Mason, Lucy Hunt, Stephanie Kempson, Sam Collier, James Harrison, Holly Stoppit, Raissa Pardini, Alfie Tyson-Brown, Nicola Jones (for the title!), Culture Recordings and The Crofters Rights.

The *Outlier* team would also like to thank the friends, families, partners and housemates who have supported us over the past year.

Very special thanks to Loveday and Lucy.

PREQUEL

MAL: When I think about it now, it doesn't feel like a dream.

It feels real still, as though I could turn around a corner
and just find myself back there.
As though time and place were the same thing.
And my phone might start ringing, and it's one of them,
so I'd walk down the lane to meet them,
we'd pick up where we left off
and keep on walking…

There's not much else to do but walk around here.
The sky is painfully big, but our worlds were small, our lives little.
So when we found each other in the muddle of it all,
found some quiet understanding in the grey and green
that feeling of belonging was addictive.

In all this space and sky and sheep and grass
and dearth of people, when you find someone you *know*
within seconds of meeting them, you cling on tight
'cause it's rough sometimes, feeling so low in a place
that could be the cover of a chocolate box.

Where you could walk out of your house
and within minutes be far, far away from another human being
but somehow not feel lonely.

It was the small towns that always made me feel lonely,
with faces that taught me familiarity was not a synonym for friendliness;
balding, beer bellied men who clung to the side of the bar every night,
that girl who went crazy and poured kettle water over her brother,
who everyone knew sold drugs to the kids down the rec.
These places aren't so idyllic after you've been around them for a little while.

But we found somewhere.
It was shabby, but it was ours.

That's the thing about love, isn't it?
Sometimes it's not in great nick,
the edges are frayed and you've
spilled wine all over it
and it's *gross* and rundown.

But it's still yours,
so you hold on even tighter.

Ama, Oskar, Lewis and Me.
Ama, Oskar, Lewis and Me.

It was like a mantra,
The one thing that fell into place like we're told things are supposed to.

I want to tell you about them.

And to tell you about them I have to go back.

GIG SPACE

MAL: Hiya. How are you?

My name's Mal, and I want to tell you a story. It's a true story. It happened to me and to my friends. Sometimes this story is hard to tell, so I've brought some friends with me to help me tell it. This is Jakabol!

Now, we're not actors, but, and the people we're talking about are real – so we're going to do things a little differently. These guys aren't going to go full method, they're not going to act or become other people… they're just kind enough to be lending their voices to help our story come alive. I'll introduce you.

This is Maz on violin – she will be the voice of **HOLLY**.

Here we have Owen on the drums, Owen's going to be **LEWIS**.

This is Emmy on the harp and flute, she's **AMA**.

And finally, on guitar, this is Joe. He'll be taking on **OSKAR**.

JOE: Uh – just so you know I *do* have a drama degree sooo…

MAL: Oh, nice. How'd you do?

JOE: Cheeky little 2:1.

MAL: *Nice.* So that means you can multi-role right? Lovely stuff. So, Joe will not only be our guitarist, he will be the voice of **OSKAR** and miscellaneous party people. We also have animations by the brilliant **CHRIS HARRISSON**.

Now, to tell a story we need a time and a place.

So… Devon. 2011. I'm eighteen – think I can still pull that off.

*(The band humour **MAL**.)*

So… Joe, what does a party sound like in 2011?

(Joe plays something unexpectedly raucous.)

MAL: No no no no, no! More chilled. More like…everyone is just sitting around, smoking their dad's hash.

(Joe plays a funky riff – the band joins in with gusto.)

MAL: I love it when they do that!

So…

THE PARTY

I'm at a house party!

Nowadays I am a party pro,
but I never used to be any good at them.
All these people breathing in one enclosed space,
It can be suffocating

but you grow to love how all the assorted bodies
learn to work together for a few hours,
making sense of the comforting strangeness of being.

This house party is in Buckfastleigh.
You'll know somewhere like it.
It's one of those *nothing* places.
Nothing happens here,
it's a whole heap of *nothing*,
with *nothing* but houses, hedges and teenagers with
nothing to do.

I don't know whose house this is,
all I know is that it is *trashed!*

There's thick bong smoke hanging like bunting
in what I think used to be a kitchen,
but it's hard to tell 'cos someone has fallen through the table,
so now the wood sticks up all jagged edges and harsh lines
and this guy is in hysterics! Laughing!

Laughing like this broken table is the funniest thing he's ever seen.
His jeans are down by his knees and a girl I used to go to school with
is attempting to use loo roll to dab at the blood
where his skin has kind of slid off his thigh,
like a label that hasn't been completely peeled off the back of a CD case.

(The band gradually stops playing as they grimace at the scene.)

The loo roll is ineffectual and just sticks to the wound
but he's alright.

Uh… Do you think he's alright?

(Beat.)

BAND: Yeah, yeah, he's alright!

MAL: *(Slightly unconvincingly.)* He's fine…

(The music starts back up again.)

I've realised a few things happen when you take drugs.
You get prickly and hot,
like stars are on your skin,
and you want to talk to everybody
and you are suddenly *so interesting!*
And nothing hurts for a little bit.

I came here with Holly. I love her.
My most enduring friend since year seven.
She's the one who keeps me stable.
She is strong and sensible and full of love.

Recently she's found a girl who makes her feel
like she was told men were supposed to make her feel.
And they've slipped off together

So I'm adrift at this party feeling fuzzy
looking for familiarity in the fog.

> **PARTY GOER (JOE):** Mate can I have a bottle?
> Do you have a bottle, though?

There are some boys in the bedroom who I recognise.
They were in my brother's year at school.
They're the ones who didn't get out of here,
still live with their mums, have jobs in Spar
and always hang about with people much younger
than themselves.

But their bodies are starting to betray them,
bellies softening, straining against tight t-shirts.

These boys are looking for a bottle to make a shotty,
and they're looming over this girl like

> **PARTY GOER:** Do you have a bottle?

The girl is Ama.
She looks utterly bemused by their very existence.
She's pale and dark at the same time, so small that her arms wrap
all the way around her legs over to the opposite shoulder.
The hippy cloth fabric of her dress makes her look like a little
jellyfish.

She spots me, smiles. Her smiles are rare, and so feel like she's shared
with you a secret,

> **AMA:** I didn't know you were going to be here!

"Neither did I."

Her smile understands, eyebrows raise a quarter inch –

> **AMA:** Always the way.

Suddenly the party is bearable, and I want to stay.
Ama.
We've known each other since we were small, barely formed.
Thrown together by hippy camps and circumstance.

Ama tells me Oskar is here.
She tells me in an annoyingly knowing way like

(Flirty.) Oskar is here you knoooow!

And I'm like *"yeah I know"* in a way I intend to be casual but blatantly is anything but.

(To the band.) Oh guys…Guys, the way I like Oskar is absolutely disgusting and mushy and gross. Like, the idea of him makes me go…

(Emmy and Maz play beautiful, romantic dreamy music as the animation forms love hearts and swirls.)

But the reality of when he actually walks into the room is more like

(Joe and Owen bust out heavy metal – loud, stressful, panicky music as the animation becomes jagged and frenetic.)

Once I told him I couldn't ride a bike,
And he said he couldn't ride a bike either!!!!
And I was like OMGGGG, we're like, basically, the same
person!!! Right?!?!

(The band looks skeptical… but encouraging!)

I think he likes me though, really.
That makes me like me, too.

Someone downstairs turns the music up
and the house begins to vibrate in rhythm.

                    AMA: I feel like that is our cue to go and have "fun"

She says fun like it's a dirty word and I love that about her.

We move together through sweaty rooms and smoky corridors
Oskar's eyes shine green and glassy.

                    OSKAR: Hello, you…

He grabs me by the waist,
I feel like spaghetti on a fork
And we dance
And he is beautiful

And we are spinning and spinning and spinning and I hope we never stop!

AMA'S ROOM

After the party, we go to Ama's house.
Ama's bedroom is an escape plan.
always stuffed full of people who have nowhere else to go.

It's dusty – ashtrays full of burned incense, roached rizla packets, curled and moistened by multiple mouths.
Ama sits now, quietly bundled in blankets clutching a mug of tea and a rollie rolled so tight and thin that it looks like a lollipop stick.

Oskar is drunk, gesticulating wildly with a bottle of white rum in one hand.
His movement takes up the whole room. Jet black hair falls in all the right places to look like one of those photos of artistically tortured adrogynous boys that teenage girls share on their tumblr.

He's telling us about his future plans:

> **OSKAR:** I will either be a spectacular failure
> or a poetic genius.
> No in betweens.
> No half measures.

He takes a triumphant swig from his bottle before falling into that squirmy, sweaty slouch of someone too drunk to be in their own body.

Ama smiles at him like a world weary mother

AMA: *(Teasing.)* You are always the most and least hopeful person in the room at the same time.

Greedy.

Ama never seems ruffled, it's like she lives in slow motion.
Oskar shifts drastically between high octane flights of fancy to treacly solemnity then back again. Somehow, they seem to even each other out.

Oskar does a thumbs up at me, then Ama, then back to me,

then drifts into the gap between asleep and awake that only drunk people can find.

AMA: I don't think he'll write his masterpiece any time soon.

"Nah."

She smiles at the floor.

"Oh, hey! Lewis is back soon."

Ama looks up and nods, her eyes softening as a smile spreads across her whole face

AMA: *Yeah. I can't wait. I can't wait!*

Birds are beginning to emerge just outside the window and the house creaks.
Ama's expression changes at the creak.
Softness steels and eyes shoot suddenly to the door
which flies open with such force paint falls off the wall –

AMA'S DAD (OWEN[1]**):** *get the fuck out of my house, are you doing drugs?*

Ama's dad is not a large man.
He's wizened, doubled over.
His hair a grey, cloudlike shriek.
He is often drunk.
Usually in a dozy way, the kind that tries to join in the party
before slowly nodding off in front of the TV.
Benevolent, soft spoken.
But tonight, there's an energy to him that I recognise.
Something sad and unwieldy

AMA'S DAD: *get the fuck out of my house with your drugs and alcohol in my fucking house!*

Oskar and I scuttle past him, down the stairs
into the sharp slap of the early hours.

---

[1] These lines are "drummed", and the words themselves come up as animation in time with each drum hit.

I'd glimpsed Ama's face behind us as we left
Leaving her in the distance.
She didn't look scared or shocked.
She looked bored.
Tired.

AMA ALONE

There's always a moment
after everyone has left
where the silence feels buoyant.
The space that once had bodies
in each crevice
looks alien.

The floor is a hole,
is a place she skirts
the edges of.

Alone, Ama blinks,
cracks knuckles, licks lips
stares at things that are not there,
her mouth twitches into an absent smile.

She breathes in,
the air still thick, heavy
with the smell of other people.
She thinks about how their mouths move
so freely and easily.

She pulls on rubber gloves,
begins to clear the debris.
Begins to clean up
the mess we made
as though it were her own.

She's used to this.
The ebbing of night to day.
Moon melting like butter
into the sky.

Bleaching and scrubbing
until the sun beats down
on window pane.
The reverse of an alarm clock

Alone, Ama's
Nights are days
And days are nights
but none of it matters anyway
A day is a day is a day is a day
And alone her days just melt away.

(Violin and harp play an outro to this poem. Eventually, the guitar picks up a walking melody. Something youthful and full of hope.)

We walk home together,
Oskar and I, across the divers field,
where the trees open out
and moon reflects off the murky
stream below.

Our footsteps are silenced by dry mud and grass,
Hands bump together flirtatiously…
You know what I mean.

He helps me over a gate
and we're suddenly on tarmac again,
which feels less safe than the silence granted to us by nature.

We stop under the orangey glow of the street light outside my house

Oskar doesn't live far from me
but I ask him if he wants to come in and stay

And he says yes.

Ohhh yeahhh!

*(The band gives **MAL** a thumbs up.)*

GIG SPACE

(**MAL** *checks if anyone in the band needs to tune. While they're tuning,* **MAL** *asks them about parties – what's the favourite party they've been to? What makes the perfect party? Each night this is different depending on who needs to tune and who's free to chat.*)

LEWIS AND THE TORTOISE

MAL: So we're going to Totnes now, a few weeks later. And I'm at another hous–

       DRUNK MAN (JOE): *(Interrupts with conspiracy theories and nonsense.)*

MAL: I'm at a house party.

       DRUNK MAN: *(Continues being tedious.)*

MAL: It's shit.

       DRUNK MAN: Thing is, right, Mel… It's Mel right?

MAL: It's Mal.

       DRUNK MAN: Yeah, Mel. Yeah. So thing is…*(Tedium fades out.)*

MAL: Sometimes I think I'm too nice.

Putting up with these endless rounds of conversations about fuck all. There's only one reason I'm at this party. Lewis is back. Owen, you ready to be Lewis?

OWEN: Yep!

MAL: Great! First, let me tell you about him.

When I first met Lewis he literally popped up out of nowhere. A brisk morning, bodies strewn sleeping across the kitchen floor as I sat on the counter-top examining a mysterious bruise on my shin. Suddenly these giant blue eyes and huge grin appear, peering through an open window. He brandished a punnet of strawberries which he ceremoniously shoved into my hands crying –

       LEWIS: Serotonin!

MAL: Before scrambling through the window frame onto the counter next to me. It was as though a cartoon character had leapt out of a TV screen to hang out.

I'd never seen someone so optimistic so early in the morning! so warm and open and *interesting* for a change. I'm so used to *these* conversations.

DRUNK MAN: *(Interrupts with more conspiracy theory chatter. Loudly.)*

MAL: Beige conversations.

Conversations that are just filling up the space where life should be.

DRUNK MAN: Mate tell you what this is just like Skins!! Wait, you're a
poet right? Can you freestyle? Wait, do you wanna hear my rap?

MAL:

"Mmmm sounds… Great.
I just need to… Go somewhere else… For a bit.
Oh, but do you know Maz? She *loves rap!*

(To Maz.) Sorry, mate.

I go to the garden.

It's the only place you're guaranteed space in these tiny cul-de-sac
type houses.

And there he is.

Broad shoulders, pale t-shirt, skinnier than I remember but Lewis.
Sat cross legged on the lawn next to Ama. I watch them for a second
in their quiet, tender bubble. The way their bodies circle into each
other. Ama is categorically *not* a giggler. But as Lewis leans even closer,
placing a hand under her small chin, tilting her head to look into his
eyes, something in her melts away.

I turn to sneak off. But Lewis spots me and waves me over.
Scrambling to his feet, he smiles that big smile and envelops me in a
hug that lifts me off the ground.

Ama's face is flushed and bright as the three of us grin at each other,
then fall into our familiar formation, sitting in a circle on the floor.

Lewis regails us with stories
And because it's Lewis, we know it's all true:
Learning fire poi from a tattooed Colombian girl he met on the
beach.
The week spent cutting down bananas as work to secure board
with a small family in Australia.

He comes alive when he tells these stories. Uses voices, bounces up on his knees to add emphasis.

Life *happens* to Lewis, it never seems to stop.

"But are you happy to be back? To all this!"

I gesture to the dark silhouettes of the trees that bloom
like spilled inkwells across the sky
The red plastic slide at the bottom of the garden.
The particular blue chill.

"That debbonair Devon air!"

                    LEWIS: Well. I missed this at least.

And he places a hand on both of our heads to drag our hair down into our faces in a clumsy, affectionate pawing motion.

Oskar wobbles into the garden, folding himself into grass with pint cans of Carlsberg wedged under each armpit that he places carefully in the middle of us,

                    OSKAR: You found him then. He's back.

Then jumps to tackle Lewis. They've always played like puppies. This time Lewis protests, shoves him off. He digs into his jacket pocket and delicately produces a match box.

                    LEWIS: I want to introduce you to my new pal.

Lewis carefully pushes the match box open

                    OSKAR: Mate! Is that a tortoise?!

And it totally is. There she is…

a tiny tortoise.

A little life sat snug in her cardboard kingdom.

He tells us she's called Mavis. He saw her crawling around in a bucket in Morocco, trying to get out but failing to find her footing. She would tumble back, scramble, tumble, scramble, tumble.

So he hoiked her out, smuggled her home in a matchbox across continents.

We look at her now, so tiny, green-grey with a little pink mouth snapping at nothing.

Lewis always does stuff like this, he saves birds from drowning in streams,
Finds boxes of abandoned kittens, nurses them to health himself. But Mavis is the strangest thing yet. He holds her so delicately that we all hold our breath to watch her crawl on his gently shaking hand.

Mavis. Completely alien in her surroundings, casting around for familiarity.

Mavis. I guess she's one of us now.

(The band plays a segment of their song Redfern. Everyone is invited to dance.)

ROMANCE

MAL: I have a question.

What do you think is the most romantic place in the world?

(The band plays a sexy melody.)

Maybe… Paris? In the Springtime? Hmmm?

Or… Venice after dark?

Nah…

For me…

(Beat.)

it's *Wilkos*.

JOE: *(Singing.)* Oh yeeeahh!

MAL: Newton Abbot Wilkos. Next to the bus station.

Oh! That red and white sign

Oh! That tatt you don't need but

want as soon as you see it!

Oh! Wilkos!

There's no S but you add it anyway,

Is it plural, is it possessive?

I don't know, I don't care, I *love Wilkos*!

Where we can pretend to be normal for a bit.

Oskar and I have been together

In a real way now for three months!

I mean, we always had a thing, but now it's a *real* thing, y'know?

And when we walk through Wilkos it feels realer than ever.

It's not the serotonin rush sexy or the chemical carnality we're used to. It's not even bouquets or chocolate boxes.

It's cuddles by the cable ties,

JOE: *(Singing.)* Cable ties, baby!

it's buying flumps for 60p
Remember flumps?!

JOE: *(Singing.)* I remember flumps!

It's this beautiful mundanity.

It's being so familiar with another body
that even paint pots and light bulbs and towels
seem poetic somehow.

Oskar buys me a mug that says

"Live Each Day With Love In Your Heart"

JOE: *(Singing.)* Live every day! With love in your heart

Live every day, with lo–

It's kinda awful

(Joe looks offended.)

And totally tacky.

But *he* is lovely
So I want to walk around Wilkos forever.
Hand in hand, looking at nothing, in the daytime.
When he is sharp eyed, witty and kind.

Wilkos is so romantic
that I forget why it is we came to town in the first place.

PICKING UP IN DEVON

It starts:
You call a friend who is a friend
of a friend with the stuff
they're either always posh hippies
or scabby and rough
they're boring and tedious
but the prices are low
you don't have to be friends
but be courteous, though.
You meet at the rec
or somewhere equally tame
and save the dealer in your phone
under their surname.

It's all pretty innocuous,
pretty safe,
pretty sound.

But as your tastes advance
You can go underground
quicker than you thought
things get sketchy and dark:

You no longer pick up in the
rec or the park.

You meet in a flat
near your old secondary school.

What you thought at first was
pretty edgy, pretty cool
dissipates pretty quick
when you spot dry blood up the wall

But again,
you get used to the acrid and sticky.

You start to learn that junkies are
Not to be trusted, nah – they're tricky.

Don't buy from them. Try someone
clearer instead. Someone who knows their
chems and supplies a wide spread.
Basically, the aim is: Don't wind up dead.

I know it sounds dramatic, but Devon is a county of extremes.
Yes, it's a place of fields, farms, and cream teas.
But within an hour you can be in a Newton Abbot crack den,
then home watching TV in bed again.

After Wilkos we go to a little flat on the outskirts of town to pick up.

I stay in the living room while they go to the kitchen. The living room
has one armchair in it. Nothing else, no other furniture, just one
armchair. Who has only one arm chair?

Weird.

When Oskar comes back out he's hazier, floaty. The gleam has gone
from his eyes.

We head back to his, have a smoke. He drifts into lanquidity,
sentences muffled.

I feel a bit abandoned when he does this.

I open my laptop, check Facebook. Lewis has uploaded a photo of
Mavis, a pair of tiny toy sunglasses placed on her shell, he's written
the caption "Schoolz out for Summer !!!" it's pretty funny.

I turn to Oskar to show him, but he's already dropped off into a deep sleep.

BAD PARTY

A couple months later, Holly drives me to another house party. Near town.

And pulls up to one of those cookie cutter council houses.
Square, white and in need of repair.
The kind of house you know that the carpet is going to be a state before you even walk in the door.

The windows are glowing blue and green and a couple are leaning on the door,
necking and, if I'm not mistaken, fingering! Right there! In the driveway!

> **HOLLY:** God. You know what…I'm really not feeling this.

But I've already dropped a bomb and I'm on the cusp, that itchy, squirmy cusp of coming up.

> **HOLLY:** I think I'm going to go home.

"God, you've been so boring since you got a girlfriend! (Singing) Let's dooo iiiit Hoollyyy."

> **HOLLY:** I'm going home. Just… Drink water okay?

I bundle out of her yellow car and wave her off like Gene Kelly does to that taxi in Singin' in the Rain.

I feel a bit sick.

Like my stomach is floating a couple of inches away from my mouth but okay okay okay.
I take a deep breath.
Push past the fingering couple…
And head into the house.

(The music becomes overwhelmingly loud and chaotic.)

Noise deafening
Can only hear
Vowels.

And that noise
Kicks me into
Coming up
Quick

I don't recognise
Anyone
So I go
To the hall

Smashed Glass
Wide eyes
White lines
Green granules
Smoke in
Teeth out
Jesus Christ

Find the kitchen!
If ever you feel alien at a party – find the kitchen.
It's quieter, the shapes more familiar –
Lewis is there, faced away, swaying against the sink.

I start towards him, but Ama appears, thin fingers digging into my arm
as she pulls me back into the hallway.

Ama is smoking ANGRILY

"Why are you smoking so ANGRY?"

AMA: Mal, I'm leaving

"I literally just got here! What's going on?"

AMA: Come with me

Every time I blink, her face slips and slides about,
like a lava lamp or something

AMA: Jesus you're high. Look. Are you coming?

"But why you leaving though?"

    AMA: Lewis and Oskar are on one and I just *can't* do it tonight.

"What's wrong with Oskar?"

        AMA: You *know* what's wrong with Oskar.
        Nothing. Everything. Bullshit.
        I'm going home.

She gives me a quick hug
then she's gone.

I turn back into the kitchen.
Lewis has dry blood on his knuckles.
I turn him around, and he hugs me
with his whole weight
Slightly too long.
His body against mine feels heavy.
Not just literally.
It's like, when a child falls asleep on you
and you carry the weight of everything
They're thinking about too.
But Lewis is a man.
And he is so solid and I can feel...
I can feel how tired he is.

        LEWIS: I fucked up, Mal.

I sit him on a chair, pour him a glass of water
My hands are shaking, body radiating heat.
I ask him if he knows where Oskar is, he gestures dismissively in the
direction of the stairs
Then stares down at his swollen knuckles

        LEWIS: I punched a wall.

"Why?"

He covers his face with his hands.

"Oh hey, hey, it's okay – no worries. Just have some water, yeah?"

LEWIS: Okay.

But he doesn't. His hands drop to his lap as his
head droops, eyelids fluttering shut

I drape my coat over him, and go upstairs to find Oskar.

Oskar's head is thrashing to and fro
I can barely see his pupils
pinprick little things
And when he looks at me
He looks through me
Stuttering
Shuffling
He's a scribble of a person

I pull him into the bathroom where he collapses,
a marionette with his string cut,
against the bath as he slips from consciousness

Oskar's chest falls.
Slows
then
stops.
The door opens, I slam it shut.
Someone shouts, kicks it,
the force knocks against my head
I am reeling
and ringing
And. Oskar's not
breathing.
Or I'm.
Not. Breathing.
Or.
We're.

Not.
Breathing.

I clamber over to him and press my lips to his.
When you breathe into someone's mouth
Their chest swells like a balloon

Have you ever felt a body feel inanimate?
Feel like material?

I breathe into him like they do in films,
have no idea what I'm doing, just feel his
body bloat under my hands

Until he jerks up.

Throws up on my hands
Glares at me. Shuffles back, wheezing.
Falls straight back to sleep again.

And I am leaning against the toilet bowl.
Body buzzing.
Swaying nauseous, swirling rhythms.

I watch him sleep
and listen to the music
as it continues seeping in through the door.

(The band plays their song Argonaut as **MAL** *sits in the bathroom, shaken.)*

Interval.

GIG SPACE

*(The band and **MAL** are getting everything ready on stage. Tuning, adjusting mic stands and instrument straps.)*

MAL: Hey, Owen?

OWEN: Yeh?

MAL: So, you know after that bad party? I got these messages from Lewis. Are you ready?

OWEN: Okay, let's do it.

MAL: Thank you.

A CHAT WITH LEWIS

(On the harp, Emmy emulates the trill of a Facebook message coming in circa 2011 between each chat.

The animation supports the chat-speak, emojis and typing ellipses.)

LEWIS:

Heyyy Mal

hows you?

> **MAL:**
> yooo :) I'm good thanks
>
> you?

LEWIS:

gdgd I'm alright …

Hey

I just wanted to apologise about the party.

Bad times.

> **MAL:**
> No worries man.
> happens to us all!

LEWIS:

Yea

its not cool though.

I was a bit upset

                                                        MAL:
?

LEWIS:

Police came and took Mavis away that morning

might be facing an animal trafficking charge

          MAL:
Wtf?
That's nuts?

LEWIS:

yea

someone reported me after they saw the pics on FB…

          MAL:
Ugh
who does that?
Are you ok?

LEWIS:

I know, it is grim

y'know, could be worse i guess

puts a stopper on New Zealand plans though *sadface*

          MAL:
That's so shit man

LEWIS:

musnt grumble eh

the world will be my oyster again soooooon

also criminal records…. kinda sexy right?

lol

MAL:

Are you ok though? For real?

do you wanna meet up? could go to the pub?

Or a walk?

LEWIS:

yea soon :)

Kinda need to chill for a bit, get my head straight,

haven't been sleeping great still a bit jet lagged methinks

and i gotta make things up to Ama she is piisssssseeddd offffff

MAL:

Eeek!

LEWIS:

Eeek indeed! :O

got that sweet, sweet valium prescription for the sleeping

but making things up to Ama might take a little more time and effort :p

Oskar alright?

MAL:

(typing) …
(typing) …

Yea all good.

gonna see him in a bit actually should get ready

let me know when youre free to meet up?

LEWIS:

Will do

Be good

from your friend, the criminal mastermind

MAL:
hehe

LEWIS:

xx

GIG SPACE

*(**MAL** welcomes the audience back.)*

MAL: Okay, shall we get back to it then?

Owen – please take us away!

(Owen welcomes us back with a raucous drum solo.)

OWL & PUSSYCAT

OSKAR:
Mally Mally Malface!!!

Can I come over?
:)

MAL:

"Yeeebooiiii!"

Since the party, things have changed a bit.
Time has warped. Ama is usually busy with Lewis.
When I do see her, she seems distracted,
sitting in her room suddenly feels like an intrusion.
She says she doesn't want Oskar coming over
anymore.

AMA: He just always gets way too trashed.

So Oskar and I are alone
Mostly it's fine.
Sometimes it's great!
We'll talk until it's light, get smashed, dance in the kitchen.
And we watch endless poetry videos on YouTube,

hatching plans to leave town, find somewhere that's ours, to write and be

together against the world.

Cosy little chrysalis where nothing can touch us and no one else matters.

I buy him a notebook, owl and the pussycat on the cover.

On the inside, I write him a small poem, telling him that

his story should be told. Underneath I copy down a quote from Jack Kerouac – his favourite.

When I give him the book, he holds it close to his face and reads slowly.

> **OSKAR:** "One day I will find the right words.
> And they will be simple."

He beams at me. When he looks at me like that,

I still feel like my chest could burst.

He tells me no one has believed in him before like I do.

And that that is special. And I feel special. And we are special.

> **AMA (TEXT)[2]:** hey mal have you heard from lewis?

> **MAL (TEXT):** no sorry x

So the good days. They are so good.

But some days are bad days,

From the moment he opens the door to me, I can always tell.

There's something in the hunch

of his shoulders, the absence in his eyes.

On these days we sit in his bedroom, and I realise how small it is.

His childhood bunk bed stripped of covers, the pimpled damp on his walls

and his mum yelling downstairs.

He's almost a full man, living a whole life in a box room.

The bad days feel bottomless.

He smokes stuff off foil, put stuff up his nose –

---

[2] Animation that appears projected above the stage.

no fun or exploration, just a need to sink into nothingness.

So, I encourage him to come to mine instead,
where we can sit in the warm clutter of my room,
and watch videos, huddled under the same duvet,
safe.

OSKAR:
I bet it feels *amazing*.

We're watching *Trainspotting*. Again.

OSKAR:
I mean come on, you'd want to try it wouldn't you? Just once?

"I don't think this film is supposed to be an advert for heroin…

Everyone literally looks like absolute shit!"

OSKAR:
You must be curious though?

I shrug, burrow deeper into the duvet, try to think of a way to change the subject.
To not have this same conversation again.

OSKAR:
I just think it would be interesting to try.
I've done basically everything else, it's kinda like… the next step?
Anyway, it's not like I'd get addicted or anything.

"It's not like people plan to get addicted. Like they wake up and go – oooh y'know what? I think I'm going to get addicted to heroin today ho ho ho!"

OSKAR:
Ho ho ho?

He laughs and pulls me in, rests his chin on the top of my head. I hesitate. What I want to say could throw us into a bad night. It can happen so fast – I say one tiny thing wrong and he flips.

But I say it anyway.

"And after what happened with your dad. You know how much it can mess someone up."

OSKAR:

Maybe it'd help me understand…

We sit in silence. Watch Ewan McGregor sink into the carpet.

OSKAR:

Shall we watch something else? All gets a bit bleak from here.

"Yeah. You pick something.

do you want a cheese toastie?"

Oskar turns to me, puts hands on both my shoulders and stares into my eyes with a piercing, sober seriousness.

OSKAR:

Mal. You have to understand something about me.

There is *never* a time I don't want a cheese toastie.

AMA (TEXT): hey mal can you call me? lpeas
please**

LITTLE BLUE PILLS

Here's a truth I never knew:
Of all the scary things in the world
One of the most terrifying is being in a room
With a person you love
And being completely alone.

AMA (TEXT): mal???

That's what it does,
This brown, sticky mass
Whose glamour oozes out of
Films and music videos
It robs a person of their themness
So they are just a nodding mass on your sofa

We already knew this happened by the sea.
Those brown towns scarred by the memory of their former glory.
Where ones weakened by life washed up and ended.

It happens in the green places too
It starts with little blue pills
That sing you to sleep
Then crystallized powder
To bring you back up
And cans of the stuff
To fill in the gaps
And days become nights
And nights become days
And then you're away
And you're gone
From yourself
You are missing
No stealth
Here
Just
Little blue pills
And can upon can
A smoke and a drink and
A bedtime at noon

LEWIS

MAL: Lewis never went travelling again.

He was cleared of the animal trafficking charge, but the time it took was enough to send him spinning off his axis. Lewis always needed trajectory or he'd get lost. He couldn't slow down without stopping.

Because when he stopped, he couldn't sleep. And when he couldn't sleep, his mind was cavernous and cruel. That blue tide is too much for one person to battle, and he slipped out of reach. Lewis spent his last few days in his room, disconnected, sleeping too much but still not enough.

Lewis died and the local papers said he was troubled. That he had a history of substance misuse and mental health problems. They chalked him up as a hopeless case.

But he was my friend. He was our amazing, kind, weird, loving, generous friend. And his eyes were blue. And he loved trees, and nature, and books, and Terry Pratchett, and smiling and climbing and flaking out of commitments, and apologising with a pasta bake, and music and dancing and living and living. He loved living. He loved living.

(The band reprise Redfern. A moment of reflection, as the animation cycles through the things Lewis loved to do. The music builds, it's emotional, rich and beautiful. The song ends abruptly, before it has a chance to reach its natural conclusion. The notes ring out, we feel an absence. We sit in the silence for a moment until **MAL** *is ready to continue.)*

FALL OUT

Holly drives Oskar and I to the funeral. She speaks gently, reassuringly. Oskar gets loaded in the back seat. Drinks two cans of special brew on the twenty minute journey.

        HOLLY: We're here. Are you ready?

As I step out of the car I feel like I'm inflatable
Like I have drunk gallons and gallons of water
So much that I am full to bursting
Then that water
Turned to air
So I am inflated and heavy and all wrong.

Ama isn't here.
Since we heard, she hasn't answered the phone or the door.
I'll see her around town sometimes, in a shop or smoking a cigarette
if we talk, it's like talking to someone who can't see you.
If you don't speak to her first, she could just walk right through you.

Oskar leans on me, he smells of metal.
I can't look at Lewis' parents. Someone's parents
Should never have to be at their funeral.

The room is horrifically inoffensive and bland
With two doors, one to walk in, one to walk out
To keep the endless parade of death streamlined.

At the wake we stand in the garden and get
softly drunk. Kids, who don't understand the grief,
chase each other around the pub garden, laughing.
Oskar nods off on the picnic bench.

HOLLY: What the fuck is he on?

The cuffs of Oskar's jacket rise up as he slouches further down the bench
revealing the puffiness of his inner arms
I reach over, pull the sleeves down, the motion makes Oskar shift his position
and he rests on me
Like a baby.
Holly stares at me
And I say it, for the first time:

"I think I need to leave."

(The band plays Porto. **MAL** *looks as though she might leave the stage.*

But she doesn't.)

AMA'S ROOM IN AUGUST

When someone dies, everything feels piercingly significant.
Every coincidence is a sign,
Every day an opportunity,
But as the meantime turns back into days
you lose your promises
as the Spring turns to Summer.
And I'm still here.

Ama has started letting Oskar back into her room,
Or rather – she doesn't have the energy to keep him out.

Her room is different, almost painfully clean. Fresh white paint barely covering the doodles on her walls that show through. Like ghosts. The only picture left up is a photo I'd never seen of her and Lewis. Printed on A4 paper, their faces are pressed together. Ama's laughing, eyes shut tight. Lewis grins, one arm stretched to take the photo, the other circled around her shoulder.

She barely speaks these days, and the silence is a mist between us. Clouding the room.

When we first arrive, we talk quietly. But as more cans are opened or wine poured, Oskar and I fall into a rhythm – we slip into the language of couples – accidental in-jokes and bickering. His voice builds in volume as he drinks, Ama winces. We are the only mess in her room. Suddenly we don't fit together.

I know she doesn't leave the house anymore. Each time I've come over, her shoes are collapsed in the exact same position.

When I go to the bathroom – the stinging smell of bleach and lemon lingering in the air – I notice pharmacy bags screwed up in the bin.

We sit – a fractured circle on a too-warm summer's night. Ama holds her hands in her lap, they're pink and blistered from cleaning products. Oskar is drinking spirits again, almost shouting.

OSKAR: It's fucked really though isn't it?

He's talking about not getting his dole money this week. He slept until four and missed his appointment.

AMA: You already said that.

"It's bad obviously, yeah. I tried to call you."

Ama rolls her eyes and I feel embarrassed.

Oskar heaves himself up and stumbles to the toilet. There's a void in the room left in his absence. She clicks about on her laptop, puts on a song.

AMA: Nothing's going to change if you keep acting like this is normal.

"What?"

AMA: That's the fourth time he's gone to the loo in an hour. Every time he comes out more drowsy. What do you think he's doing in there? Because he's not pissing.

"I know, but, it's like... He'll get there. You know? I'm just trying to make sure he's okay."

AMA: You're just covering for him. Every time he fucks up you're there like a...fucking...Cushion.

"I mean... I love him—"

AMA: If you love him like that. Nothing's going to change.

Oskar shuffles back in, twitching his fingers, he goes to sit back down.

AMA: Shut the door.

He turns, but it seems to unbalance his equilibrium and he tumbles slowly. It's almost comical how treacly slow he falls, hand knocking a full wine glass off the bedside table.

Red liquid splatters across Ama's photo, seeps into the smiling faces. She stands up fast.

I realise I haven't seen her standing up in a long time.

She is so thin, all angles.

Her skin is different.
Her face and her neck.
All different.

AMA: Get *out*.

I grab Oskar, who's laughing, a shrill, strangled, alien laugh.

"I'm sorry Ama, he's just—"

AMA: I know what he is.
A waster.
He's the one who's still here and he's *wasting* it.

I pull Oskar towards the door, and we stumble downstairs. Ama stalks behind us, her dad in the living room stands to watch, silent and swaying.

AMA: Don't come here anymore. I mean it.

OSKAR: Fuck it, don't want to anyway. You're mental.

He throws his words like grenades, then stomps out of the door. I look back at Ama, she avoids my eyes, staring into the patterns on the carpet. I go to hug her but she steps back.

"I'm sorry, I have to go and see he's alright…."

AMA: Don't come here anymore, Mal. I won't be here.

So…

I leave.

LEAVING OSKAR

And we're alone again.
There are still good nights, but they're different. They shift into something
sludgy and slow. We'll drink a bottle of wine each and watch whatever's on TV, curled around each other on a small sofa like we're one being. Our chrysalis has become gooey nothingness. A numb, comforting routine.

But the bad nights now. They're *bad*.
Nonsensical arguments, things broken.
I go to the shop, come back and find him shooting up in my bedroom.
Or he'll go to the loo a little bit too long, come back and nod, nod, nod.

It happens so slowly that the bad begins to seep into everything and seem normal.
But the very worst nights. They're the nights where Oskar cries in my lap. Apologies and clawing hands. He cries, says he wants to stop but then, minutes later, he does it all again.

And these patterns fall into months.
The months become a year.
And I am still here.

One morning I wake up before him. Begin to clean.
I stack sticky empty glasses, throw burned, balled-up tin foil in a
plastic bag.

That's when I see it.
Under the bed.
Scraps and ribbons of paper and card,
wrinkled from being beer drenched and dried. The smiling face of an
illustrated cat torn right down the middle.

I scoop up the remnants of the notebook. Cover ripped and curled.
The ink of my poem, a jumbled, distorted blur. The Jack Kerouac
quote just splintered confetti, sticking in clumps on the carpet.

"Oskar. What happened to this?"

OSKAR: Sorry I needed roach…and stuff.

"But I got you this. I got it for you."

OSKAR: I'll get another one.

He turns to the wall. I stare at the back of his head, his pale shoulder
falling as he slips back to sleep. And it's the apathy of it. The
nothingness. The realisation that a part of him has become so distant
that he's just…the shape of someone I used to know.

I go to the bathroom and wash my hands. It's all I can think to do. I
wash them under a too hot tap. I look in the mirror and I can see it. I
can see it in my body and my face and my skin.
I can see it's time to go.

BRISTOL

So I ripped myself away
Into somewhere new
I pulled away so hard that my wounds
Were still open by the time I made it

To Bristol.
Where I'd howl and scratch and convulse
because leaving an addict brings

Its own withdrawal.

I'd stay up till 5am, trawling through old text messages.

I read them so much I knew them by memory.

Every email to Ama bounced back.

Her phone number was one long tone.

Holly kept checking in after helping me move.

Online, I'd see her happy photos, her found family, and bright hair turning

Purple and blue and red. I saw her becoming who she was always

Supposed to be

So I took strength. Began to cobble together a life,

took the plans Oskar and I had made for two, and repurposed them for one.

I wrote poems about feelings,

So the feelings felt more manageable

And people told me their stories too

And we all wrapped our wounds in words.

Sometimes the words were clumsy.

Or messy.

But they were mine.

So I built and I built

And I cried and I worked and I slept, actually slept.

And I found a home

where I could laugh and love again.

The tiny threads of Devon dwindled.

I'd hear tales of Oskar

Attempting to get sober, falling again, being arrested, getting better, getting worse

The never ending saga of the boy with green eyes

Who I loved. The boy who disappeared, even though

he was still standing right in front of me.

Somehow two years had past

And I was bigger and more than ever before

When suddenly, one day, Oskar's face appeared on screen
Older, heavier, bearded, but those eyes were there
and his messages unfurled on screen:

OSKAR: Mal?

Hi.

Please talk to me.

Okay, you don't have to talk to me.

I just want to let you know I'm better.

I'm so much better, Mal.

I'm in a dry house in Exeter. I'm back at college.
They said I'm dyslexic, so I'm getting support as well.

It's good. I'm going to be the person I should have always been for you.

"Hi."

OSKAR: Hi Mal.

Thank you for talking to me.

I'm going to get better Mal.

"I really hope so. It's good to hear you're doing

Something good."

OSKAR: I really am Mal.

Can we meet?

Ok, we don't have to.

But thank you for talking to me Malface.

I'm going to get better. :)

Smiley face.
One kiss.

MISSED CALLS

I have five missed calls on my phone and I know why.
When my phone rings a sixth time I let it ring out and text back

"Heya bit busy, everything ok??"

HOLLY: "Call me back ASAP."

And suddenly I'm on a train
Whizzing past fields
And more sky than I can handle
And I am too big but also too small
And too much of everything at once
And I step off the train and Holly is there
And she bundles me into her arms
And her girlfriend does the same
And holds me so tight
But I am still spinning and spinning
And I want to stop and get off.

We go to the funeral.
A tiny sprinkling of people
I haven't seen in years
Stand awkwardly out the front, smoking and squinting in the sun.

Ama, Oskar, Lewis & Me.

It's just me now.

I can't go to the wake, every face is a reminder
that I'll never see Oskar's again.

Holly takes me to Wetherspoons, we drink
horrible pints in the prickly summer heat,
She takes me back to the station
I quietly throw up in the crosscountry train
Toilet. And I go home.

Back in Bristol
I go out and I smash against everyone and everything

I am afloat.
I am some kind of debris floating around, untethered.
Unanchored. Alien.

I go to a pub where I don't know anyone and just let
my body drift, get flung about by the music and the booze
And back into the blue pills and the white.

I drift
and I drift

Until I drift to the right place, one night

and meet this band

who are loud
and lovely
and needed
and they help

me to drift back to writing

and it feels good again

It feels like something worth doing

It feels like

I am bringing ghosts back to life

So I write

And I write

And I write

And I write

And I write

And I write

And I write

GIG SPACE

MAZ: And do you remember the first thing we wrote together?

MAL: *Smash cut smart suit, smash cut dress….*

*(The band and **MAL** unite to perform their song Baku. It's heavy, raucous and melodious – an impassioned meditation on realising that you can be a different person every time you wake up, and how that realisation can be simultaneously chaotic and cathartic.)*

MAL: We're nearly at the end of our story, or rather – we're nearly up to date. But Maz, I have this voicemail from Holly. Do you think you could read it for me?

A PHONE CALL

HOLLY:

Hey babe. I hope you're okay. Haven't heard from you in ages but I always like reading your Facebook statuses…ALL of them! Even though you're constantly bitching about Devon which I find a BIT rude but y'know.

Anyway, I think you should come back for a bit. I know you probably don't want to.
But honestly, come and see my new place.
Me and Kelly, we'd love to have you stay. I think sometimes you have to come back to a place for it to stop seeming so scary?

All I know is you should come back for a bit. Call me back, okay? I have something to tell you!

THE TERRACE, ASHBURTON

MAL: There was this summer where Lewis got really into Buddhism. As you do. And he started making his own mantras. One day we were all sitting in the divers field. I'd been trying to write a poem about the four of us and failing miserably and Lewis, in his most sage voice, says *"it's impossible to make sense of something that isn't finished yet"*. Obviously we all took the piss. Then Oskar said *"I don't think anything is ever really finished though, is it?"* And Lewis was like, *"well then, guess you never have* *to make sense of anything. And nothing ends. I think that's a pretty good way of living."* And grinned, closing his eyes as he turned his face to the sun.

I think about this moment on the train journey back to Devon, where Holly has something to tell me.

I've been on this route so many times – I can map it out. The crumbs of Temple Meads, Taunton's featureless station, the spread of fields, greens and yellows, it passes through the muddle of Exeter's rails, stations we used to sit at for hours waiting for the two carriage trains that never turned up, a brief glimpse of sea in Dawlish – splash of blue amongst the grey, the blocky, inert buildings in each town and city we'd found, where Oskar had sometimes waited for prescriptions, or therapists, or help that never came. Because he really did try. Sometimes. He tried so hard to be alive. And I pull up to Newton Abbot station, this little station with its chipped brown stone, barely changed except now it has new barriers that I bet kids can still jump over.

Holly is by her bright yellow car, waving me over – I comedy run towards her, arms outstretched. That's when someone else steps out of the car. Small but strong and smiling.

AMA: Hi Mal.

There's this hill ten minutes from where we grew up
It's steep, and from the bench at the top you can look
Down at the whole town.
That's where we go to sit.

Ama is blonde now. She tells me she
Started to find the dark oppressive.
She tells me everything about her was changing
so she wanted to run with it.
I tell her I know what she means.

And we just talk. It's nice.
She talks me through her absence
How, for a moment, she couldn't even see herself,
how she was sick of it.
So sick that she made the decision to find a remedy,
Spent a couple of years in clinics and wards

figuring out who she deserved to be – someone happy.
We talk about her new life overseas,
teaching children and feeling things she never thought
she could.
She says sorry for disappearing. I say it's fine.
We're here now. We're alright.

And the sky does what it does
Goes from light grey to deep blue
And eventually
We talk about them.

We talk about how this will always be sad,
How every time the phone rings
we wonder who has died.
We talk about the strangeness of knowing
That when a man walks in front of us
With a blue rucksack casually hanging
Off his shoulders, it will never be Lewis.
And how somewhere a dusty book of poetry might sit
Forever on a shelf that might have
Been picked up by Oskar.
And how they are past tense and always
Will be and our memories with each of them
Belong only to ourselves now.

What I find most comforting
is just that they *were*.
Something tangible.
Something mundane and simple.
That they existed for other people too
that someone saw Lewis in Tesco
Dithering over what ready meal to buy
his brow furrowed,
How he gripped his trousers between forefinger
And thumb in concentration.
How Oskar might have moved seats on a bus

to let an old person sit down
Or smiled at a baby in the street.
He loved babies.
We talk of

Empty Rum Bottles
Blue & Red Striped Jumpers
Benches on Hills
Punnets of Strawberries
Fields Full of Sheep
Broken Bicycles
Half Burned Incense
Roached Rizla Packets
Sharpie Scribbled Walls
Super Noodle Sandwiches
Tortoises in Match Boxes

These fleeting mundanities of life
That prove that they lived.

We talk until the
memories lose their meaning
Until the sky is ink and our town is
Polka-dotted with the pinprick
of bedroom lights glowing in the distance.

AMA: Feels like we're really far away from it.

But we're not really.

AMA: Yeah. I was invited to this house party. Do you wanna go?

Nah. I kind of like the quiet. I kind of want to just sit here.

AMA: Yeah. Me too.

God. It's so small isn't it?

Yeah.

It's tiny.

Ends.